M000210342

Collins

easy learning

French

Pronunciation

HarperCollins Publishers
Westerhill Road
Bishopbriggs
Glasgow
G64 2QT

First Edition 2013

Reprint 10 9 8 7 6 5 4 3 2 1 0

© HarperCollins Publishers 2013

ISBN 978-0-00-749192-6

Collins® is a registered trademark of
HarperCollins Publishers Limited

www.collinslanguage.com

A catalogue record for this book is
available from the British Library

CD recording by Password Ltd

Typeset by Davison Publishing
Solutions, Glasgow

Printed and bound in China by
South China Printing Co. Ltd

Acknowledgements
We would like to thank those authors
and publishers who kindly gave
permission for copyright material
to be used in the Collins Corpus.
We would also like to thank Times
Newspapers Ltd for providing
valuable data.

WRITTEN BY
Caroline Smart

EDITORS
Gerry Breslin
Phyllis Buchanan
Lisa Sutherland
Thomas Widmann

FOR THE PUBLISHER
Lucy Cooper
Kerry Ferguson
Elaine Higgleton

Contents

Guide to the Audio

This book is accompanied by an audio CD. The CD contains the following tracks:

1   Introduction
2   Points about French
3   Inside the mouth
4   Consonants
5   Vowels
6   A and B
7   C and D
8   E
9   F, G and H
10   I, J and K
11   L, M and N
12   O and P
13   Q and R
14   S and T
15   U, V and W
16   X, Y and Z
17   Liaison
18   The alphabet and spelling
19   Practising words
20   Goodbye

Track 1: Introduction
Meet our two presenters.

Track 2: Points about French
Things to bear in mind when speaking French and how French differs from English.

Track 3: Inside the mouth
A tour of the different parts of the vocal tract used for speech.

Track 4: Consonants
An explanation of how consonant sounds are made. Find out which ones are voiced and which ones are voiceless.

Track 5: Vowels
An explanation of French vowel sounds – front, back and nasal vowels.

Track 6: A and B
- a: la, plat, animal
- *nasalised* a: an, sans, chambre

- b: bon, bien, Bordeaux
- bs/bt: absent, observer, obtenu

Track 7: C and D
- c + e, i, y: centre, cinéma, cygne
- c + a, o, u: carton, combien, cuisine
- ch: chanson, chercher, chic

- d: de, dans, droit
- *final* d: pied, grand, blond
- *with liaison*: un grand artiste, un grand homme

Track 8: E
- e [e]: été, jouer, les, chez, et, pied
- e [ɛ]: père, mer, billet
- e [ə]: le, demain
- eu: peu, deux
- eur: peur, fleur
- *nasalised* e: en, lent

Track 9: F, G and H
- f: fois, frère, fromage

- g + e, i, y: gens, gilet, gymnaste
- g + a, o, u: gare, golf, guerre
- g + *consonant*: glace, grippe
- *final* g: sang, long
- *with liaison*: de long en large
- gn: montagne, gagner, vigne

- *mute* h: l'homme, l'histoire
- *with liaison*: en hiver, trois hommes
- *aspirate* h: la hauteur, le haricot

Track 10: I, J and K

- i: il, vie, finir
- i + *vowel in same syllable*: bien, camion
- *nasalised* i: timbre, vin

- j: jeudi, jardin, juin

- k: kilo, kilomètre, klaxon, ticket

Track 11: L, M and N

- l: lait, lettre, louer, balle
- il(l): travailler, soleil, famille, fauteuil

- m: ma, mercredi, midi
- *nasalising a vowel*: chambre, faim
- m + *mute* e: rhume, dame, Rome
- *double* m: femme, homme
- m + *another vowel belonging to next syllable*: ami, amour, numéro

- n: nuit, Nice, nager
- *nasalising a vowel*: centre, volcan
- n + *mute* e: une, jeune, lune
- *double* n: bonne, panne, anniversaire
- n + *another vowel belonging to next syllable*: animal, fenêtre

Track 12: O and P

- o: hôtel, numéro, rose
- o + l, t, r: bol, votre, orange
- *nasalised* o: non, bon
- o + u: nous, cours, rouge
- o + i, y: roi, voyage

- p: père, pour, poisson
- *silent* p: temps, champs, compte, sept, corps
- *silent final* p: trop, coup, sirop

Track 13: Q and R

- q: que?, qui?, quel(le)?, quoi?

- r: radio, réserver, riche

Track 14: S and T
- s: salut, six, salade
- s *between two vowels*: visage, rose, maison
- *silent final* s: Paris, jus, la voiture, les voitures
- *with liaison*: les enfants, ils ont

- t: ton, trois, totalement
- *silent final* t: mot, lait, billet
- *with final* e: petit-petite, haut-haute
- ti + *another vowel*: information, infection, confidentiel, substantiel, infectieux

Track 15: U, V and W
- u: une, lune, vu
- ou: rouge, nous, cours
- *nasalised* u: un, parfum

- v: voilà!, vous, vrai

- w *sound made by* o + *another vowel*: ouest, soir, voiture, royal, loyer,
- w *sound made by* u + *another vowel*: Suisse, suis, sueur, Suède

Track 16: X, Y and Z
- x [ks]: fixer, expérience
- x [gz]: exiger, exhibition
- x [s]: six, dix, soixante [six chambres, dix voitures]
- x [z]: deuxième, sixième, dixième
- *silent final* x: doux, prix, toux
- *with liaison*: aux États-Unis, deux élèves

- y *like* i: y, stylo, type
- y: essayer, joyeux, payer
- *nasalised* y: sympathique, syndicat

- z: zéro, zone, gazeux
- *silent final* z: chez, riz, nez

Track 17: Liaison
- un grand ami, les amis, aux amis
- deux heures, ces enfants

- un bon ami, un grand amour
- chez eux, dans une minute
- très intéressant, bien entendu
- elle est allée
- en hiver, bien entendu
- *no liaison: after* et – vingt-et-un, trente-et-un
- un mot intéressant
- Paris est …, Louis est…
- toujours en France

Track 18: The alphabet and spelling

- a b c d e f g h i j k l m n o p q r s t u v w x y z

- **comment ça s'écrit?** (*how do you spell it?*)

- **ça s'écrit p, e, t, e, r** (*it's spelt p, e, t, e, r*)

- **j point cook arobase yahoo point co point u k** (*j.cook@yahoo.co.uk*)

- **caroline arobase agilebooks (tout un mot) point co point u k**
  (*caroline@agilebooks (all one word).co.uk*)

- **notre site web, est double vay, double vay, double vay point Collins point co point uk** (*our website is www.collins.co.uk*)

Track 19: Practising words

This track includes a selection of words that are spelt the same in English and French (give or take a couple of accents). Practise saying them as 'Frenchly' as possible!

Track 20: Goodbye

French Pronunciation

Into the face of the young man who sat on the terrace of the Hotel Magnifique at Cannes there had crept a look of furtive shame, the shifty hangdog look which announces that an Englishman is about to talk French.

The Luck of the Bodkins P G Wodehouse

If you've ever struggled with your French pronunciation, wondering why you don't seem to be able to produce the right sounds, then *Collins Easy Learning French Pronunciation* will help identify where the problem lies.

As a nation we are often uncomfortable speaking French, squirming in embarrassment at the sounds that come out of our mouths. Instead of trying to understand how written French corresponds to spoken French, we tend to stick to the rules we know for speaking English which are not actually the ones we need to capture authentic French sounds.

There is a saying that to really understand another person you should walk a mile in their shoes. Well the same could be said of speaking another language. You need to spend time inside a native speaker's mouth. Not literally, of course! Once you realise you aren't placing your tongue where a French person would, it can help you reproduce the correct sound.

Fortunately pronouncing French is quite straightforward once you know a few basic rules and learn how the French use their vocal tools – mouth, lips, tongue, etc.

But before we begin to examine each of the various sounds, we look at how French and English differ and what effect this has on the way French is spoken.

We explain:

- How the vocal tract works
- What a consonant is
- What a vowel is

The second part of this book lists an A to Z of all the letters describing in detail how each one is pronounced wherever it might fall in a word or when it is in a particular letter combination.

Points about French

- French is very different to English. French is a Romance language (like Italian and Spanish) coming mainly from Latin. English is more of a mishmash of languages including Anglo-Saxon, French, Latin, even Arabic and Hindi (*shampoo* and *curry* both come from India).

- French has gender. Nouns are either masculine or feminine and words describing them have to reflect this. This is known as 'agreement'. Often an **e** is added to make a masculine word feminine, which can affect how the word is pronounced. This is something to remember if you are female, and talking about yourself.

- The endings of many French words are not sounded, even though they might end **d**, **t** or **s**, such as **grand**, **filet** and **Paris**. In English they are: *grand*, *fillet*, *Paris*.

- Although the usual way to make something plural in French (like English) is to add an **s** (**chat**→**chats**), the ending still isn't pronounced because of the rule about most final consonants (**d**, **t**, **s**, etc) not being pronounced. So both the singular word for **chat** (*cat*) and plural word **chats** (*cats*) sound exactly the same. In English you nearly always hear a final *s*.

- Some endings in French are not pronounced as you might think. For instance, the **-ent** ending of verbs corresponding to 'they' (**ils parlent**, *they speak*) sounds exactly the same as the ending **-e** (**il parle**, *he speaks*).

- Although French word endings are often silent, if the next word starts with a vowel, then sometimes that ending is pronounced, but tacked on to the following word (known as liaison). So in **les chiens** (*dogs*) you don't hear the final **s** of **les**. But with **amis** (*friends*), then the **s** is heard as a **z** sound (**le**[z] **amis**).

- French uses various accents (marks above or below letters). They actually provide helpful information, either how to pronounce a letter or to differentiate words with the same spelling but different meanings.

- In English we always emphasise ('stress') one syllable of the word. We say MACKintosh, not mackINtosh or mackinTOSH. French words do not behave like this. Any or none of the syllables may be stressed according to the context.

- It's often said that the French move their mouths more energetically when they speak, whereas English is pronounced more 'lazily'. You'll need to round your lips much more fully than you're used to for words such as **tu** and **vous**.

- The vowels **a**, **e**, **i**, **o** and **u** are usually nasalised when followed by a single **n** or by **m**. The sounds **n** or **m** end up more of a vibration rather than a distinguishable sound.

- French **r** sounds nothing like English *r*. It's more of a gargle at the back of your throat, or the rasping *ch* in the Scottish word *loch*.

- In French, a statement is turned into a question simply by lifting the pitch of the voice at the end. In English you tend to switch words round: *You are sad* (statement) to *Are you sad?* (question).

- Unlike English, French has two ways of addressing someone: using formal **vous** (polite *you*) and informal **tu** (familiar *you*). You have to remember to match them with the correct masculine or feminine endings depending on the person you are speaking to: **vous êtes content(e)?** (*are you happy?*).

Getting inside your mouth

When you learn to speak, you tend not to think about how the language works. You simply absorb the sounds and patterns it makes and then reproduce them. It is only natural to think along the lines of your own language and assume that another language has the same patterns and sounds. Many of the mistakes people make when they start out learning another language are caused by this. As soon as you become aware of differences and look for patterns in the new language then these 'mistakes' should become a thing of the past.

Before we begin to look at French pronunciation, it's worth finding out how we produce sounds. This is where we need to get inside our mouths.

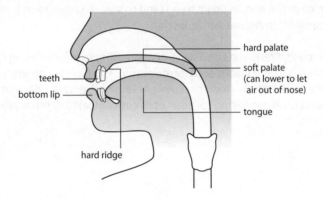

The vocal tract

The vocal tract is essentially the space from your 'voice box' or larynx (where your Adam's apple is) to the lips. It also includes the nasal cavity which produces nasal sounds.

Your voice box is at the top of your windpipe. Two bands of tissue inside the larynx are called vocal cords (or folds). Air coming out of the lungs causes these cords to vibrate to produce sounds. You can feel these vibrations by placing your hand on your Adam's apple while saying 'ahhh'. A sound produced with the vocal cords is known as 'voiced'. Sounds produced with just the breath are termed 'voiceless'. You can have two consonants produced in the same way, but one is 'voiced' (such as **b**) and the other is 'voiceless' (such as **p**).

The gap between the cords is known as the glottis. A glottal stop is often used instead of a *t* in English (referred to by some people as 'dropping your *ts*'), as in *'bu'er'* for *butter* or *'you go' a car?'* (*you got a car*). It's made by closing the glottis completely and then releasing it explosively. Avoid using glottal stops when speaking French. French **t** may be silent at the end of a word, but it is never 'dropped'.

It is the tongue, teeth and lips that allow us to make a wide range of sounds. A lack of any of these is going to make it difficult for someone to speak clearly.

The space inside your mouth is one of the most important parts of the vocal tract. Its size, shape and acoustics can be varied by the movements of the tongue, lips, cheeks, teeth and palate. Essentially these are what you use to produce sounds.

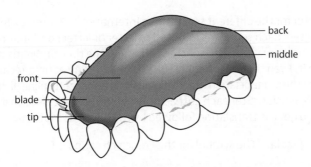

The tongue is a particularly flexible instrument. The tip and the edges can be moved independently and the entire tongue can move forward, backward, up and down. You can make your tongue very pointed. When it is at rest in the mouth the blunt end is known as the blade. Where you place your tongue can vary in different languages and just being aware of this can help you produce the right sound. For instance an English *t* is pronounced with your tongue tip pressed against the hard ridge just behind your top teeth. Now move the tip of your tongue forward to touch your teeth and say *t*. This is where a French **t** is pronounced.

The lips control the size and shape of the mouth opening through which speech sound is passed. Lips can be tightly rounded, stretched wide or in a relaxed open position.

Different sounds of letters

When you are taught the alphabet, you learn that there are five vowels (*a, e, i, o, u*) and the other letters are consonants (*b, c, d, f, g* and so on). However these aren't enough to cover the full range of sounds needed. So combinations of letters are used to convey any missing sounds, for example *th, ch* and *sh*. This is where you start to see distinct patterns forming in each language.

Problems arise when one letter combination isn't mirrored in another language. In English the *ch* letter combination gives a tch-sound as in *church*. In French **ch** produces a sh-sound (as in *shout*). But try telling that to an English-speaking mouth! Its automatic reaction on seeing **chat** would probably be to pronounce the English *ch* sound (and probably even sound the final **t** which is silent in French).

In order to cater for the different sounds, the International Phonetic Alphabet (IPA) was devised. Each sound (as opposed to letter or letter combination) is given its own unique symbol. It's worth spending some time familiarising yourself with it. Even though it might look rather daunting at first, it can really help you to get the pronunciation exactly right. Many paper and online dictionaries include the IPA version after each entry. So if you look up 'chocolate' in a French dictionary, you get the translation followed by the IPA transcription:

chocolat /ʃɔkɔla/ (The symbol for the French **ch** sound is ʃ)

A GUIDE TO THE INTERNATIONAL PHONETIC SYMBOLS USED FOR
FRENCH SOUNDS

The International Phonetic Alphabet gives each sound its own unique symbol to eliminate any confusion about what sound to make. Below are the letters and their IPA symbols. Notice how one letter can have a variety of sounds. Vowels are highlighted in grey.

French letter	IPA symbol	examples and comments
a	[a]	la, Paris, château
nasalised a	[ã]	an, chambre
ai	[ɛ]	mais, naître
au	[o]	haut
b	[b]	bon, robe

c	[k]	carton
	[s]	centre, ça
ch	[ʃ]	chanson, chercher
d	[d]	de, dans
e	[e]	été, jouer, les, chez, pied
	[ɛ]	père, restaurant, billet, jouet, neige
nasalised **e**	[ã]	en, temps
nasalised **ei**	[ɛ̃]	plein
	[ə]	le, je, petit
eu	[ø]	peu, deux
eu	[œ]	peur, meuble
f	[f]	fois, neuf
g	[g]	gare, gorge
	[ʒ]	gens, gilet, gymnaste
gn	[ɲ]	montagne, gagner
h	*silent*	mute **h** behaves like a vowel: **l'hôtel**
	silent	aspirate **h** ['] behaves like a consonant: **le haricot**
i	[i]	vie, lit
	[j]	viande, mieux
nasalised **i**	[ɛ̃]	vin, timbre, matin
j	[ʒ]	je, jeudi
k	[k]	**k** is only found in loan words: **kilo, ticket**
l	[l]	lait, sel
il(le)	[j]	fille, soleil
m	[m]	ma, femme
n	[n]	nuit, bonne
o	[o]	hôtel, numéro
	[ɔ]	bol, votre, orange
nasalised **o**	[ɔ̃]	nom, mon
ou	[u]	vous, genou
oi	[wa]	oiseau, poivre

p	[p]	père, frapper
ph	[f]	photo, pharmacie
q	[k]	quatre, cirque
r	[ʀ]	restaurant, trente
s	[s]	salut, poisson
	[z]	rose, visage
t	[t]	ton, quitter
u	[y]	une, tu, vu
	[ɥ]	suis, tuer
v	[v]	voilà, ouvert
w	[v], [w]	wagon, week-end **w** is found only in loan words
x	[ks]	taxi, fixer
	[gz]	exemple, exister
	[z]	deuxième
y	[j]	yeux, voyage
	[i]	stylo, type
nasalised y	[ɛ̃]	sympathique, syndicat
z	[z]	zéro, gazeux

Accents and marks

Unlike English, French uses accents to give information on pronunciation and differentiate confusable words.

Acute The acute accent is used only on **é**. It goes up to the right. It means a more closed kind of **e** (as in your tongue is closer to the roof of your mouth), more like *may* than *met*: **été**, **bébé**, **thé**.

Grave The grave accent slopes down from the left. It is found on the letters **è**, **à** and **ù**.

It is used on **à** and **ù** to differentiate words with the same spelling but different meanings. It does not tell you how to pronounce the letters.

- **a** (*has*) as opposed to **à** (*to*)
- **la** (*the*) as opposed to **là** (*there*)
- **ou** (*or*) as opposed to **où** (*where*)

It is rarely used with the letter **e** for distinguishing purposes. One instance is in **dès**, as in the phrase **dès que possible** (*as soon as possible*), where it is spelt with an accent so as not to confuse it with **des** (*some*).

A grave accent on **e** tells you to pronounce it [ɛ] as in **père**. It's found in words that end in a consonant and silent **e** (e.g. **-ce**, **-ge**, **-me**, **-re**, **-te**): **pièce** (*room*), **siège** (*seat*), **crème** (*creme*), **père** (*father*), **diabète** (*diabetic*).

Many masculine adjectives ending in **e** plus a consonant gain a grave accent in the feminine form:

- **discret→discrète** (*discreet*)
- **premier→première** (*first*)
- **cher→chère** (*dear*)

Cedilla The hook beneath the letter **ç** is known as a cedilla. It tells you to give the **c** a soft [s] sound when it would normally be pronounced [k] because it is followed by **a**, **o** or **u** which are 'hardening' vowels: **français**, **garçon**, **reçu**

Circumflex The 'hat' or circumflex over a vowel generally indicates a letter has disappeared over time (usually **s**). The English equivalent has often kept the missing *s*: **pâte** (*paste*), **forêt** (*forest*), **île** (*isle*), **côte** (*coast*), **août** (*August*), **coût** (*cost*).

A circumflex is also used with **û** to differentiate short words:

- **du** (*of the*) and **dû** (*owed*)
- **sur** (*on top of*) and **sûr** (*sure*)
- **mur** (*wall*) and **mûr** (*ripe*)

Dieresis Two dots (called Umlaut in German) over a vowel tell you to pronounce it separately from the vowel next to it: **Noël** (*Christmas*), **Citroën**, **Gaëlle** (a girl's name). Otherwise you might pronounce the two vowels as a single sound.

Likewise, a dieresis can avoid confusion. **Aigüe** is the feminine form of **aigu** (*sharp, shrill*). Without the two dots a reader would assume the **u** was just there to keep the 'hard' [g] sound and therefore not pronounce it separately.

Contraction (also known as elision)

When **je** is followed by a word beginning with a vowel or mute **h** it shortens to **j'** as in **j'ai** (*I have*), **j'habite** (*I live in*). A similar thing happens in English with *it is* and *he is* becoming *it's* and *he's*. In English this contraction is optional (you can say *he is* or *he's*), in French it isn't (you can't say **je ai**). The same thing happens with:

- **le** and **la**: **l'arbre** (*tree*), **l'idée** (*idea*), **je l'ai vu** (*I saw him*)
- **de**: **d'eau** (*some water*)
- **je, ce, ne**: **j'aime** (*I love*), **c'est** (*it is*), **n'est pas** (*is not*)
- **me, te, se**: **je m'appelle** (*my name is*), **il t'a vu** (*he saw you*), **s'amuser** (*to enjoy oneself*)
- **que**: (**qu'est-ce qu'on mange?**) (*what are we eating?*)

> Note that **qui** (*who*) is never shortened.

Consonants and Vowels

What is a consonant?

A consonant sound is one that is made by blocking the breath either completely (*d*, *p*, *t*) or partially (*f*, *l*, *s*); whereas a vowel sound is made by an uninterrupted flow of air and different mouth shapes.

English and French consonants are not too different. Just a few require you to move your tongue into a slightly different position to capture the real French sound.

There are two basic ways of making consonants: voiced and unvoiced. Voiced consonants involve the vocal cords. Unvoiced consonants involve no vibration of the vocal cords and use just the breath.

The different sounds of French consonants include:

Stops where the breath is stopped and then released to create the sound as in **p** and **b** (using the lips), **t** and **d** (with the tip of the tongue against the inside of the top teeth), and **g** and **k** (using the back of the tongue and the hard palate).

Fricatives where the breath is forced through a narrow opening as in **f** and **v** (between the bottom lip and top teeth), **s** and **z** (between the tongue and hard ridge behind the top teeth), **ch** [ʃ] and **j** [ʒ] (between the tongue and the roof of the mouth) and French **r** [ʀ] (between the back of the tongue and the back of the throat).

Nasals where the soft palate is lowered to release air out of the nose (**m**, **n**).

As you would expect, if you are not aware that French letters are pronounced differently, your mouth is going to opt for the English 'default' position. It may take a little time to train your brain out of its English groove.

French consonants to be on the lookout for include:

c – This has a hard [k] sound when followed by **a**, **o** or **u**: **calme** (*calm*), **comme** (*as*) or **cuisine** (*kitchen*). It has a soft [s] sound when followed by **e** or **i**: **cent** (*hundred*), **cinéma** (*cinema*). The word **concert** (*concert*) includes both sounds.

g – This can also have either a hard [g] or a soft [ʒ] sound. Followed by **a**, **o** or **u** it is [g]: **gare** (*station*), **gorge** (*throat*), **guide** (*guide*). Followed by **e** or **i** it is [ʒ] as in *massage*: **gentil** (*kind*), **gilet** (*waistcoat*).

h – Is always silent.

j – Has the same [ʒ] sound as a soft **g**: **je** (*I*), **janvier** (*January*), **juin** (*June*).

r – Is a gentle gargle at the back of the throat. It is similar to the *ch* ending in Scottish *loch*.

You will find details of all the consonants in the **A–Z** section.

Silent consonant endings

In English words, the 'rule' is that if a word ends in a consonant (*s*, *t*, *d* and so on), then the ending is sounded. In French, apart from a few exceptions, the opposite is true, so be careful not to pronounce French endings, even if your mouth is itching to do so!

We have already learnt that an English *cat* definitely has a *t* at its tail but a French **chat**, however, does not (even if there is more than one cat, **chats**, neither the **t** nor the **s** is sounded). Endings that are normally not sounded in French include: **pas**, **mot**, **riz**, **prix**, **grand**, **trop**. The A-Z section goes into more detail and lists any exceptions.

You do hear final consonants in loan words, which are foreign words that have been imported into French (in other words, borrowed). So while the final **s** in *repas* (*meal*) is silent, it is sounded in the loan word *bus*.

Feminine endings

Adding an *e* to a word (usually to make it feminine) causes a final silent consonant to be pronounced: **petit** (*little*) becomes **petite** (the final **t** is now sounded).

Other regular spelling changes to adjectives that affect how they are pronounced are:

masc	fem		masc	fem
-	-e		-eur	-euse
-ef	-ève		-eux	-euse
-eil	-eille		-ier	-ière
-eil and	-eille are pronounced		-if	-ive
	the same (except in		-il	-ille
	poetry etc)		-on	-onne
-er	-ère		-ot	-otte
-et	-ette, -ète			

What is a vowel?

> A vowel is a sound made without any obstruction of the airway.
> Try saying *a, e, i, o, u*. Was anything obstructing the sound?

Vowel sounds start with vibrations in the vocal cords (and are therefore all voiced). The different sounds are made by changing the shape of the mouth using the tongue and lips.

Vowel sounds depend on:

- How high the tongue is in the mouth – high, mid or low.
- Which part of the tongue is highest – front, middle or back.
- Whether the lips are rounded or stretched wide.

In describing speech sounds, people sometimes refer to 'pure' vowels. It's not a moral thing! Some vowels are the same throughout their duration, while others sort of slide around as you say them. Generally French sounds are more pure than English ones. English vowels often slide into diphthongs. A diphthong is where there are two different vowel sounds run together. In an English word like *by*, you start with the sound *a* and slide into an *ee*: *ba-ee*. You might be tempted to let vowels slide in French, but try to train your mouth out of the habit and avoid:

- **les** becoming *lay-ee*
- **des** becoming *day-ee*

Listen to and watch French native speakers and imitate their style. This is easy now in the age of the internet: foreign television, YouTube, maybe even Skype?

French vowel sounds

> Rounded vowels are where your lips are rounded, [o] being the most obvious. Other sounds like [i] involve the lips being spread.

French vowels sounds are made from the usual **a**, **e**, **i**, **o** and **u** (and in many cases **y**), plus letter combinations such as **au**, **ei**, **ou** etc. Factors including where a letter falls in a word or whether or not it has an accent can affect how it is pronounced. This is why it is very useful to learn the IPA symbols. These show you exactly which sound is required.

There are twelve French vowel sounds (though one has more or less gone out of use), four nasalised vowels (again, one has fallen out of use) and three semivowels.

French has five rounded vowels which means they are pronounced with rounded lips, particularly **u** [y] as in **tu** where lips are tightly pursed. This is a high front vowel (meaning it is pronounced high in the mouth towards the front). Its high back counterpart [u], as in **vous**, is also pronounced with tightly rounded lips, but at the back of the mouth. As soon as you see a rounded vowel, your lips should get into position even before you pronounce the letter before it.

Although each vowel is covered in detail in the **A–Z** section, it is useful to see where they are pronounced in the mouth in relation to each other. The table on the next page shows you where in the mouth (back, front, high up or low down) each one is sounded. The tongue is forward for the front vowels and pulled back for the back vowels. The **e** [ə] as in **le** sits in the middle of the mouth with the tongue almost flat. Of all the vowels, it is the most relaxed.

As the tongue and vowels move down in the mouth, the spreading and rounding of lips slacken off as you reach the two bottom [a] and [ɑ] sounds. As mentioned previously, French vowels are much purer than English ones. To keep them pure, keep your mouth and tongue in the same position for the length of the sound. Maintaining this tension will avoid the vowel sliding into a diphthong.

POSITION OF VOWELS IN THE MOUTH SPACE

roof of mouth

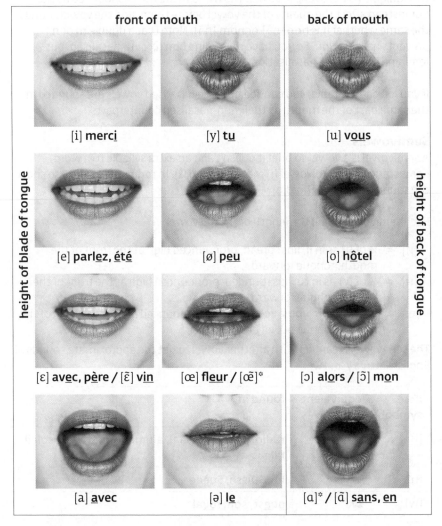

front of mouth   **back of mouth**

height of blade of tongue   *height of back of tongue*

[i] merc<u>i</u>   [y] t<u>u</u>   [u] v<u>ous</u>

[e] parl<u>ez</u>, <u>été</u>   [ø] p<u>eu</u>   [o] h<u>ô</u>tel

[ɛ] av<u>e</u>c, p<u>è</u>re / [ɛ̃] v<u>in</u>   [œ] fl<u>eur</u> / [œ̃]*   [ɔ] al<u>o</u>rs / [ɔ̃] m<u>on</u>

[a] <u>a</u>vec   [ə] l<u>e</u>   [ɑ]* / [ɑ̃] s<u>an</u>s, <u>en</u>

bottom of mouth

* *These vowel sounds have gone out of use: [ɑ] has been replaced by [a] and [œ̃] has been replaced by [ɛ̃]*

Nasalised vowels

A nasalised vowel is produced by lowering the soft palate and allowing air out of the nose as well as the mouth as you release the sound. Vowels followed by a single **n** or **m** are generally nasalised. The phonetic symbol for nasalisation is the squiggle (tilde) over the vowel. The **n** and **m** are not pronounced as such but instead affect the quality of the vowel before them, and the vowel sounds the same whether it is **non** [nɔ̃] or **nom** [nɔ̃]. Note that a double **m** or **n** prevents nasalisation. So you have masculine **bon** (*good*) – nasalised, but feminine **bonne** – no nasalisation.

If you look at the table, you can see how the nasalised vowels are sounded in the same part of the mouth as their non-nasalised counterparts.

Semivowels

A semivowel is a vowel so brief it doesn't add an extra syllable to a word. For instance, the semivowel [j] is a shortened [i]. In **radio**, the **i** in **io** is so short the sound ends up **yo**: [ʁadjo].

Each semivowel is half the length of the full vowel:

[j] = ½ of [i] as in **il**, lips spread, pronounced high at the front of the mouth, tongue forward

[ɥ] = ½ of [y] as in **tu**, lips rounded, pronounced high at the front of the mouth, tongue forward

[w] = ½ of [u] as in **vous**, lips rounded, pronounced high at the back of the mouth, tongue pulled back

The semivowels team up with another vowel to get the approximate sounds of English letters *y* and *w*:

IPA symbol	equivalent letter	found in
[j]	y	rad**io**, pap**ie**r, spéc**ia**l, alumin**iu**m, trav**ai**l, sol**ei**l, f**ille**
[ɥ]	w	l**ui**, S**ui**sse, S**uè**de
[w]	w	**ou**est, s**oi**r, ro**y**al

Syllables

> Syllables are units of sound.

A word can be made up of one or more syllables:

cat = one-syllable word
cats = one-syllable word (adding a letter has not added a syllable)
catnap = two syllables (*cat* and *nap*)
caterpillar = four syllables (*cat-er-pill-ar*).

A syllable can be closed or open.

A closed syllable is one that ends with the sound of a consonant. **Toute**, **belle** and **rose** are all closed (even though the last written letter is a silent vowel).

An open syllable is one that ends with a vowel sound (even though it might be written with a silent consonant). This includes the verb endings **-s** and **-ent**.

- Closed syllable words = **lac** (*lake*), **balle** (*ball*), **gare** (*station*)
- Open syllable words = **pas** (*not*), **riz** (*rice*) and **jus** (*juice*), **tu parles** and **il parlent** (**parles** and **parlent** are considered single syllables because of their silent endings)

Wherever possible, French syllables begin with a consonant: **a-ni-mal**, **gé-né-ral**

Syllables should be divided between consonants: **al-ler**, **lais-ser**, **té-lé-pho-ne**

- The following letter combinations should not be divided: **bl** or **br**, **ch**, **cl** or **cr**, **dr**, **gl**, **gr** or **gn**, **ph**, **pl** or **pr**, **th**, **tr**, **vr**:
  trem-bler (*to tremble*), **bi-cy-clet-te** (*bicycle*), **an-glais** (*English*)
- Note that a vowel is nasalised when it's followed by **m** or **n** in the same syllable. This is why knowing where to divide French words into syllables can be helpful. In **parfum** (*perfume*) the **u** is nasalised but not in **numéro** (*number*). By dividing **nu-mé-ro** into syllables, you can see the **m** belongs to a different syllable from the **u** and therefore is not nasalised.

Intonation

Intonation is the rise and fall of the voice. In French it falls in the following instances:

- Statements: **Il est parti**. (*He has left.*)
- Commands: **Asseyez-vous!** (*Sit down!*)
- Questions beginning with a question word such as
  Qui? (*Who?*), **Où?** (*Where?*), **Quand?** (*When?*), **Pourquoi?** (*Why?*):
  Quand est-il arrivé? (*When did he arrive?*)
  Qui mange de la salade? (*Who is eating salad?*)

Intonation rises in the following instances:

- Statements that are turned into questions: **Il est parti?** (*Has he left?*)
- Inverted questions (ones made by turning the subject and verb around):
  Est-il arrivé? (*Has he arrived?*), **As-tu mangé?** (*Have you eaten?*)
- Unfinished sentences: **Mais tu sais que ...** (*But you know that ...*)

Liaison

When you hear French spoken, you hear some endings that are normally silent being sounded. This happens when they are followed by a word that begins with a vowel (or mute **h**) and is known as liaison in French. Note that liaison only occurs between words that are closely connected and form a unit such as the article and noun (**un** and **homme**), the subject and verb (**vous** and **êtes**) and so on.

> Liaison can change the sound of the final letter of a word.

Compare:

Combien d'hommes? Deux (the final **x** is silent) (*How many men? Two*)
Deu[z] **hommes** (the final **x** is pronounced [z] (see below)) (*Two men*)

The consonants involved in liaison generally include **d**, **s** and **x**. However, their pronunciation is changed so that **d** becomes [t], and **s** and **x** become [z]:

- **un gran**[t] **ami** – the **d** sounds like [t] (*a great friend*)
- **le**[z] **amis** – the **s** sounds like [z] (*the friends*)
- **au**[z] **amis** – the **x** sounds like [z] (*to friends*)

> Watch out with **h**. There are two types. One behaves like a consonant (**le haricot**), therefore there is no liaison. This is called the 'aspirated h', even though the **h** is not actually pronounced. The other **h** is mute and behaves like a vowel (**l'homme**), therefore there is liaison. A good dictionary will indicate which words begin with aspirated **h**.

There are a number of instances where liaison is compulsory:

- after words that introduce nouns: **les**, **des**, **ces**, **mon** etc. This includes numbers:

  deu[z] **heures** (*two hours*), ce[z] **enfants** (*these children*)

- between subject (**nous**, **vous**, **ils**, **elles**, etc) and verbs:

  nou[z] **avons**, il[z] **aiment**, **aimen**[t]-**ils**

- after adjectives that go before the noun: **bon** (*good*), **mauvais** (*bad*), **petit** (*small*), **grand** (*big*), **gros** (*fat*) etc:

  un bo[n] **ami** (*a good friend*), **un gran**[t] **amour** (*a grand passion*)

- after short (one-syllable) prepositions: **chez** (*at the house of*), **dans** (*in*), **sous** (*under*), **en** (*in*), etc:

  che[z] **eux** (*at their house*), dan[z] **une minute** (*in a minute*)

- after some short (one-syllable) adverbs: **très** (*very*), **plus** (*more*), **bien** (*well*), **rien** (*nothing*), etc:

  trè[z] **intéressant** (*very interesting*), bie[n] **entendu** (*obviously*)

- after **est** (*is*) and other third person forms of **être**:

  elle es[t] **allée** (*she went*)

> Keep the nasal quality of the **n** in liaison: e[n] **hiver** (*in winter*), u[n] **homme** (*a man*), o[n] **a bien mangé** (*we ate well*), bie[n] **entendu** (*fully understood*).

Liaison is optional after **pas** and **trop** and using it here can sound rather old-fashioned. Listen to how French people speak and notice when they use it.

There are instances where liaison is not allowed:

- After **et** (*and*): **vingt-et-un** (*twenty-one*)
- After a singular noun:

  un mot intéressant (*an interesting word*), **un roman ennuyeux**
  (*a boring novel*)

- After proper nouns: **Paris est ...**, **Louis est ...**
- In plural compound nouns (nouns made up of more than one word):
  salles à manger (*dining-rooms*), **cartes à jouer** (*playing-cards*).
- After **toujours**:

  toujours en France (*always in France*)

 This symbol appears throughout the book to introduce information on liaison.

A–Z

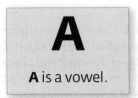

A is a vowel.

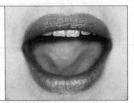

$[a]$ To make the sound: Rest the front of your tongue just behind your bottom teeth. The blade should be raised slightly. The sound is made low down in the front of the mouth. It is a front low vowel. Lips are open and quite relaxed.

French **a** is pronounced as in English *apple* and *Paris*. It has this pronunciation wherever it falls in a word.

> **la** (*the*), **ma** (*my*)
> **plat** (*flat*)
> **animal** (*animal*)

French once had another sort of **a** [ɑ] (pronounced low down and at the back of the mouth like *a* in A*r*thur). However, it's safe to ignore this distinction as few French speakers now observe it.

à   A grave accent over the letter tells you there is another word with the same spelling but a different meaning: **a** (*has*) and **à** (*to, at*). It is not telling you how to pronounce it.

Other vowel sounds
Other vowel sounds involving the letter **a**:

ai	= [ɛ] as in *Calais*: **lait** (*milk*), **mais** (*but*)
ail(le)	= [aj] as in *Versailles*: **travail** (*work*), **maillot** (*jersey*)

au	= [o] as in *hope*: **au** (*to*), **eau** (*water*), **autre** (*other*)
ay	= [ej] as in *pay*: **pays** (*country*), **essayer** (*to try*)

A 'hardening' vowel

When **a** comes after **c** or **g**, these are pronounced [k] and [g] as in **café** (*coffee*) and **gare** (*station*). The letter **a** in French (like **o** and **u**) acts as a 'hardening' agent whereas **e** and **i** are the opposite ('softening' agents).

Nasalised a

The vowel **a** is usually 'nasalised' when followed by a single **n** or **m** (within the same syllable). The **n** or **m** is not pronounced as such, it just changes the quality of the vowel into a nasal sound. The back of the tongue is pulled down as low as possible with the mouth open. The soft palate is relaxed and down, opening up the nasal cavity to let air out of the nose. It is a back low vowel as in English *Arthur*.

an (*year*)	**chambre** (*room*)
sans (*without*)	**camper** (*to camp*)

> **ain/aim** = [ɛ̃] **bain** (*bath*), **faim** (*hunger*) with the same pronunciation as in **vin** (*wine*), **plein** (*full*) and **un** (*one*)

B is a consonant.

To make the sound: Press the top lip firmly against the outside edge of the bottom lip and release. The sound [b] *uses vocal cords whereas its voiceless twin* [p] *just uses the breath.*

French **b** is like English *b*, but pronounced with a bit more energy. English *b* can sometimes lose its voicing, but French **b** is always voiced.

bon (*good*)
bien (*good*)
Bordeaux

It keeps the same quality in the middle of a word:

Décembre (*December*)
tomber (*to fall*)

A final **b** is normally silent unless it is the name of a person or place:

plomb (*lead*) (the final **b** is silent)
Job (*Job*) (the final **b** is sounded)

Double **b** is pronounced as though single: **abbaye** (*abbey*)

In loan words (words borrowed from another language), a final **b** is
pronounced as it would be in its original language:

le web (the final **b** is sounded)
le club (the final **b** is sounded)

When **b** is followed by **s** or **t** (**bs**, **bt**), the **b** is generally pronounced **p**:
absent (*absent*), **observer** (*absent*)
obtenu (*got*)

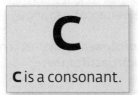

C is a consonant.

French **c** has two pronunciations. The word **concert** includes both examples:
[k] and [s]. The clue to pronouncing them lies in the letter after each **c**.

To make the sound: The end of the tongue is very close to the hard ridge just behind the front teeth, forming a narrow airway to force the breath through. The sound [s] is made with the breath whereas its voiced twin [z] uses vocal cords.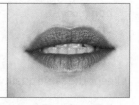

C is pronounced [s] when followed by **e**, **i** or **y** ('softening' vowels) as in English *centimetre* and *cigar*. The phonetic symbol for this type of **c** is the one also used for the letter **s** [s]:

> **centre** (*centre*)
> **cinéma** (*cinema*)
> **cygne** (*swan*)

[k] To make the sound: Raise the back of your tongue to touch the roof of your mouth and then release. The sound [k] is made with the breath whereas its voiced twin [g] uses vocal cords.

When **c** is followed by **a**, **o** or **u** ('hardening' vowels), it has the same sound as English *cat*, *cot* and *cut*:

> **carton** (*cardboard*)
> **combien** (*how much/many*)
> **cuisine** (*kitchen*)

> French [k] is not aspirated in French – in other words when you release the back of your tongue from the roof of your mouth, there is no accompanying puff of air.

C also has a [k] sound when followed by another consonant such as **l**, **r** or **t**:
spectacle (*show*), **sucre** (*sugar*), **actif** (*active*)

A final **c** is usually sounded:

> **lac** (*lake*)
> **parc** (*park*)
> **sac** (*sack*)

Exceptions include: **tabac** (*tobacconist*) and **porc** (*pork*)

Double **c** is pronounced as though single when followed by **a**, **o** or **u**:

> **occasion** (*occasion*)
> **accord** (*agreement*)
> **occupation** (*occupation*)

But if **cc** is followed by **e** or **i**, then the first **c** keeps the [k] sound and the second **c** is pronounced [s]:

> **accepter** (*to accept*)
> **accident** (*accident*)

When **c** is followed by **a**, **o** or **u**, but needs to keep the [s] sound, a hook (known as a cedilla) is added beneath it (**ç**). This tells you to pronounce it [s]:

> **ça** (*that*)
> **leçon** (*lesson*)
> **reçu** (*receipt*)

....

CH

To make the sound: The blade of the tongue is close to front of the hard palate. Lips are slightly rounded, forming a passage to force the breath through. The sound [ʃ] is made with the breath whereas its voiced twin [ʒ] uses vocal cords.

The letter combination **ch** in French has the same sound as *sh* in English *shout*:

> **chanson** (*song*)
> **chercher** (*to look for*)
> **chic** (*chic*)

Look out for the few words where **ch** has the same [k] sound as in English:
Christ (*Christ*), **orchestre** (*orchestra*), **echo** (*echo*)

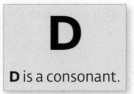

D is a consonant.

[d]

To make the sound: Press the point of the tongue firmly against the inside of the top teeth and release. The sound [d] is made with the vocal cords whereas its voiceless twin [t] just uses the breath.

English *d* is generally pronounced with the tip of the tongue against the hard ridge just behind the top teeth. French speakers tend to have the tip of their tongues resting against their top teeth which makes for a softer more Mediterranean sound. English *d* can sometimes lose its voicing, but French **d** is always voiced.

de (*of*)
dans (*in*)
droit (*right*)

In the middle of a word **d** keeps the same quality:

midi (*midday*)
vendu (*sold*)
jardin (*garden*)

A final **d** is generally not sounded:

pied (*foot*)
grand (*big*)
blond (*blonde*)

One exception is the word for **sud** (*south*). If in doubt, check a dictionary with a phonetic guide: **sud** [syd].

Double **d** is pronounced as though single: **addition** (*bill*)

With liaison, a final **d** is pronounced [t]: **un gran**[t] **artiste** (*a great artist*), **un gran**[t] **homme** (*a great man*).

E

E is a vowel.

French **e** has three pronunciations or can be silent:

 To make the sound: Tongue is forward and slightly higher than halfway up. Lips are wide (though not as wide as for [i]). Muscles around the mouth are quite tense. It is a front vowel.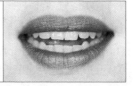

The first pronunciation is like the *e* in *fiancé*. You find it in the following:

- **e** with an acute accent: **été** (*summer*), **thé** (*tea*), **téléphone** (*telephone*)
- in the **-er** ending of verbs: **jouer** (*to play*), **manger** (*to eat*)
- in short (one-syllable) words ending in a silent **s**: **les** (*the*), **mes** (*my*), **tes** (*your*)
- in words ending in a silent **z**: **chez** (*at the home of*), **allez** (*you go*), **nez** (*nose*)
- in **et** (*and*)
- in words ending **-ied/-ier**: **pied** (*foot*), **papier** (*paper*)

 To make the sound: Tongue is forward and slightly lower than halfway up. Lips are slightly stretched (though not as wide as for [e]). Muscles around the mouth are getting less tense. It is a front vowel.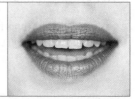

The second pronunciation is like the *e* in *ten*. This sound occurs in the following:

- **e** with a grave accent (**è**) or a circumflex (**ê**): **père** (*father*), **chère** (*dear*), **être** (*to be*), **tête** (*head*)
- **e** (without any accent) in a closed syllable (one ending with the sound of a consonant). These examples are divided into syllables: **mer** (*sea*), **hô-tel** (*hotel*), **di-vers** (*various*)
- in words where **e** comes before a final silent **t** or **ct**: **billet** (*ticket*), **jouet** (*toy*), **respect** (*respect*)

> Contrast **jouer** with its final [e] sound with **jouet** and its final [ɛ] sound.

Other letter combinations that share this [ɛ] sound are: **neige** (*snow*), **mais** (*but*), **naître** (*to be born*).

 To make the sound: Tongue is resting almost flat in the mouth. The sound is made in the middle of the mouth with lips relaxed in a neutral position. Very little effort is required for this sound.

The third pronunciation involves the least effort and is like the *e* in *over*. It occurs in the following:

- short (one-syllable) words: **le** (*the*), **je** (*I*), **de** (*of*), etc.
- when **e** is the last letter of an open syllable (one ending with a vowel sound) within a word. The examples are divided into syllables: **de-main** (*tomorrow*), **pe-tit** (*little*), **re-tard** (*delay*)

Dropping e

The [ə] sound is one that often disappears in everyday speech: **d'main** (*tomorrow*), **p'tit** (*little*), **ch'mise** (*shirt*)

However it isn't dropped if it leaves three consonant sounds running together. Therefore **e** [ə] is pronounced in the following:

appaRTeMent (*apartment*)
paRLeRons (*we will talk*)
venDReDi (*Friday*)

This rule also applies to word groups, for example: **noTRe CHambre** (*our room*). Otherwise it would be almost impossible to say!

Silent e

An **e** is silent in the following cases:

- at the end of words (even when **s** is added to make a word plural): **rose** (*rose*), **porte** (*door*), **amies** (*female friends*)
- when **e** is sandwiched between two single consonants (nasalising **m** and **n** do not count as consonants): **saMeDi** (*Saturday*), **lenTeMent** (*slowly*), **méDeCin** (*doctor*)

- in verb endings for **tu** (*you*) and **ils/elles -ent** (*they …*): **tu manges, ils mangent** (*you, they eat*), **tu parles**, **ils/elles parlent** (*you, they speak*)
- when **e** is used to keep the soft sound of **g**: **nous mangeons** (*we eat*)

Other vowel sounds

Other vowel sounds involving **e** are: **eu** as in English *hurt*: **peu** (*few*), **deux** (*two*), **feu** (*fire*)

To make the sound: Tongue is in same position as for [e], i.e. forward and slightly higher than halfway up. However, lips are rounded. Muscles around the mouth are quite tense.

- **eur/œur** is more or less the same as [ø] but occurs in closed syllables (ones that end with the sound of a consonant): **peur** (*fear*), **fleur** (*flower*), **sœur** (*sister*)

To make the sound: Tongue is in same position as for [ɛ], i.e. forward and slightly lower than halfway up. However, lips are rounded. Muscles around the mouth are less tense.

- **eil** = [ɛj] as in English *may*: **soleil** (*sun*), **vieille** (*old*)
- **euil** = [œj] no English equivalent: **fauteuil** (*seat*), **feuille** (*leaf*)

A 'softening' vowel

When **e** comes after **c** or **g**, it gives them soft [s] and [ʒ] sounds: **centre** (*centre*), **gelé** (*frozen*). The letter **e** in French (like **i**) acts as a 'softening' agent whereas **a**, **o** and **u** are the opposite ('hardening' agents).

Nasalised e

The vowel **e** is usually 'nasalised' when it is followed by a single **n** or **m** (in the same syllable), as in **ensemble** (*together*). Note that the phonetic symbol for nasalised **e** is [ɑ̃]. This means that **en** is pronounced exactly the same as **an**. The back of the tongue is pulled down as low as possible with the mouth open. The soft palate is relaxed and down, opening up the nasal cavity to let air out of the nose. It is a back low vowel as in English *Arthur*.

A double **n** or **m** stops the nasalisation of a vowel – so **en** is nasalised but **enne** (as in **antenne**) is not.

The phonetic symbol you might think belongs to nasalised **e** [ɛ̃] applies to the following letter combinations: **in/m**, **ein/m**, **ain/m**, **un/m**, **yn/m**:

vin (*wine*), **sympathique** (*nice*)
plein (*full*)
brun (*brown*)
bain (*bath*)

F

F is a consonant.

To make the sound: Rest your top teeth lightly on your bottom lip and feel them tickling slightly as you make the sound. The sound [f] is made with the breath, whereas its voiced twin [v] uses vocal cords.

French **f** is pronounced as you would in English:

fois (*time*)
frère (*brother*)
fromage (*cheese*)

In the middle of a word **f** keeps the same quality:

parfum (*perfume*)
refuser (*to refuse*)
confortable (*comfortable*)

A final **f** is usually sounded:

neuf (*nine*)

apéritif (*aperitif*)
tarif (*rate*)

In the word **œuf** (*egg*) the **f** is sounded in the singular [œf] but not in the plural
œufs [ø].

Note how a word ending **-f** in the masculine usually changes to **-ve** in the
feminine:

neuf (*m*) → neuve (*f*)
sportif (*m*) → sportive (*f*)
massif (*m*) → massive (*f*)

Double **f** is sounded as though single:

difficile (*difficult*)
différent (*different*)
office (*office*)

 With liaison, the **f** of **neuf** (*nine*) is only pronounced [v] with **ans** (*years*) and
heures (*hours*). Otherwise it keeps the [f] sound: **neu**[v] **ans**, **à neu**[v]
heures, but **neu**[f] **hommes** (*nine men*).

G

G is a consonant.

The French letter **g** has two pronunciations (like the letter **c**). The word **bagage**
contains both examples: [g] and [ʒ]. The clue to pronouncing them lies in the
letter after each **g**.

[ʒ]   *To make the sound: Press the sides of your
tongue against your top teeth to create an
airway between your tongue and the top of your
mouth. Round your lips slightly to lengthen it.
The sound [ʒ] uses vocal cords whereas its
voiceless twin [ʃ] just uses the breath.*

When **g** is followed by **e** or **i** ('softening' vowels) or the letter **y**, it has a [ʒ] sound like the s in English *leisure*:

> **gens** (*people*)
> **gilet** (*waistcoat*)
> **gymnaste** (*gymnast*)

French **j** [ʒ] shares the same sound.

To make the sound: Raise the back of your tongue to touch the roof of your mouth and then release. The sound [g] is made with the vocal cords whereas its voiceless twin [k] uses just the breath.

French **g** has a [g] sound, as in English *got*, when followed by **a**, **o**, **u** ('hardening' vowels) or by another consonant such as **l** or **r**. English *g* can sometimes lose its voicing, but French **g** is always voiced:

> **gare** (*station*)
> **golf** (*golf*)
> **guerre** (*war*)
> **glace** (*ice*)
> **grippe** (*flu*)

A final **g** is silent:

> **sang** (*blood*)
> **long** (*long*)

With liaison, a final **g** is pronounced [k]: **de lon**[k] **en large** (*back and forth*).

Double **g** followed by **l** or **r** is pronounced as though single:

> **aggraver** (*to worsen*), **agglomérer** (*to agglomerate*)

But if **gg** is followed by **e** or **i**, then the first **g** keeps the [g] sound and the second **g** is pronounced [ʒ]:

> **suggestion** (*suggestion*)

The letter combination **gu** makes a [g] sound. The **u** is silent, it simply acts as a 'hardening' agent between **g** and **e** or **i**:

> **longue** (*feminine of long*)
> **guide** (*guide*)

To reverse this 'hardening' effect and keep the [ʒ] sound of **g** when followed by **a** or **o**, then **e** is inserted (but not pronounced):

> **nous mangeons** (*we eat*)
> **Peugeot**

....

GN

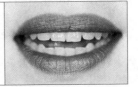

To make the sound: Flatten the front part of your tongue against the roof of your mouth and release (letting some air out of your nose). The sound [ɲ] is nasalised and voiced.

The letter combination **gn** has its own sound [ɲ] and is pronounced in a similar way to the *ny* in English *canyon*:

> **montagne** (*mountain*)
> **gagner** (*to win*)
> **vigne** (*vine*)

....

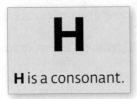

H

H is a consonant.

French **h** is always silent but has two distinct qualities. It can be either mute or aspirate.

Mute **h** behaves like a vowel: **le** and **la** shorten to **l'** in front of words starting with mute **h**:

> **l'homme** (not **le homme**) (*man*)
> **l'histoire** (not **la histoire**) (*history*)

With liaison, mute **h** behaves like a vowel: a silent ending coming before it is sounded: **e**[n] **hiver** (*in winter*), **troi**[z] **hommes** (*three men*).

Aspirate **h** acts like a consonant even though it is not pronounced:

> **la hauteur** (not **l'hauteur**) (*height*)
> **le haricot** (not **l'haricot**) (*bean*)

A dictionary will generally tell you which **h** is mute and which one is aspirate either using the phonetic symbol ['] or with an asterisk (or similar device): **haricot** /aʀiko/ (note the apostrophe) but **hôtel** /otɛl/.

H is always silent wherever it falls in a word:

> **heureux** (*happy*)
> **dehors** (*outside*)

In the letter combinations **rh** and **th**, the **h** is not pronounced either:

> **rhume** (*cold*)
> **théâtre** (*theatre*)
> **thé** (*tea*)

> Don't be tempted to pronounce **th** as in English *this* or *that*.
> The sound doesn't exist in French.

An **h** in combination with the letter **c** is pronounced *sh* [ʃ] as in *shout*:

> **chanson** (*song*)
> **chercher** (*to find*)
> **méchant** (*naughty*)

See more about this in the section about **CH**.

i is a vowel.

I has two pronunciations in French:

To make the sound: Lips are fully spread and the blade of the tongue is raised very close to the front of the roof of the mouth. This is a high front vowel. The muscles around the mouth are tense.

The first one is as in English *sheep* and French **merci**.

il (*he*)
vie (*life*)
finir (*to finish*)

A circumflex over the letter **î** generally indicates that a letter (usually **s**) has been lost over time: **île** (*isle*). It is not telling you how to pronounce it.

The second pronunciation is like the 'y' sound in **fiancé**. It occurs when **i** is followed by another vowel in the same syllable. The phonetic symbol [j] can be slightly confusing – it simply means the sound written as **y** in English *yes*.

ia: **fiancé** (*fiancé*), **dépliant** (*brochure*)
ie: **bien** (*good*), **rien** (*nothing*), **escalier** (*stairs*)
io: **camion** (*lorry*), **avion** (*airplane*)
iu: **aquarium** (*aquarium*), **aluminium** (*aluminium*)

Nasalised i

The letter **i** followed by an **m** or **n** (in the same syllable) is nasalised. The tongue and mouth position are the same as for [ε] (rather than [i]). The symbol for this is [ɛ̃]. Tongue is forward and slightly lower than halfway up. Lips are wide (though not as wide as for [e]) with the soft palate relaxed and dropped, opening up the nasal cavity to let air out of the nose.

im: **important**, **simple** (*plain*), **timbre** (*stamp*)
in: **fin** (*end*), **vin** (*wine*), **interdit** (*forbidden*), **matin** (*morning*)

A 'softening' vowel

When **i** comes after **c** and **g**, they have soft [s] and [ʒ] sounds as in **citron** (*lemon*) and **gilet** (*waistcoat*). The letter **i** in French (like **e**) acts as a 'softening' agent whereas **a**, **o** and **u** are the opposite ('hardening' agents).

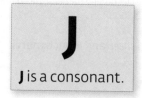

J is a consonant.

[ʒ]

To make the sound: Press the sides of your tongue against your top teeth to create an airway between your tongue and the roof of your mouth. Round your lips slightly to lengthen the airway. The sound [ʒ] uses vocal cords whereas its voiceless twin [ʃ] just uses the breath.

It has the same sound as the s in English *leisure*:

je (*I*)
jeudi (*Thursday*)
jardin (*garden*)
juin (*June*)

It keeps the same quality in the middle of a word:

bonjour (*hello*)
majorité (*majority*)
bijou (*jewel*)

g before **e** and **i** [ʒ] has the same sound. Compare **je** (*I*) and **gens** (*people*).

In everyday speech **je** is often shortened to **j'** before words beginning **p**, **t**, **k**, **q** or **f** and is pronounced [ʃ] as in English *shout*:

je te→j'te
je peux→j'peux
je crois→j'crois

....

K is a consonant.

To make the sound: Raise the back of your tongue to touch the roof of your mouth and then release. The sound [k] *is made with the breath whereas its voiced twin* [g] *uses vocal cords.*

The letter **k** is not native to French and is only found in loan words (words borrowed from other languages) such as **kilo**, **kilomètre**, **klaxon**, **ticket**.

The sound [k] in French is normally made by 'hard' **c** or **qu** (**qui**, **quai**, **quel**, **disque**). They all have the same phonetic symbol [k].

> The [k] sound is not aspirated in French so try not to let out a puff of air when you say it.

L is a consonant.

French **l** has two pronunciations:

To make the sound: Keep your tongue tip just behind your top teeth and drop the sides of your tongue so that they don't touch your teeth. The breath escapes out of the sides of your mouth as you make the sound with your vocal cords.

In English, [l] is normally light (pronounced at the front of the mouth) at the beginning of a word (*lane*), but dark (pronounced at the back of the mouth) at the end of a word (*pull*). French [l] is always light, even when it comes at the end of a word.

The first pronunciation of **l** is similar to English as in the word *love*:

lait (*milk*)
lettre (*letter*)
louer (*to rent*)

In the middle of a word it retains the same quality:

filet (*fillet*)
table (*table*)
parler (*to speak*)

A final **l** is generally sounded:

il (*he*)
sel (*salt*)
cheval (*horse*)

There are a few exceptions where the final **l** is silent: **gentil** (*kind*), **sourcil** (*eyebrow*), **persil** (*parsley*).

The second pronunciation is the 'y' sound in English *million* and **Versailles**. Its phonetic symbol is [j] which can be confusing. The sound [j] is often referred to as a semivowel. This sound occurs in the following: **ail(l)**, **eil(l)**, **euil(l)**, **ill**:

travailler (*to work*), **taille** (*size*)
soleil (*sun*), **bouteille** (*bottle*)
famille (*family*), **juillet** (*July*)
fauteuil (*armchair*), **feuille** (*leaf*)

A couple of exceptions include: **ville** /vil/ (*town*) and **mille** /mil/ (*thousand*).

Therefore double **l** can be pronounced in two ways:

- As a single **l**: **salle** (*room*), **aller** (*to go*), **ballon** (*ball*), **ville**, **mille**
- As a [j] sound when combined with an **i**: **maillot** (*vest*), **vieille** (*old*), **fille** (*daughter*)

M is a consonant.

 To make the sound: Using the vocal cords to make the sound, have your lips pressed together and let the air out of the nose.

Unless **m** is nasalising a vowel, it is pronounced as in English *mother*, but avoid releasing the puff of air that often accompanies an English *m*:

ma (*my*)
mercredi (*Wednesday*)
midi (*mid day*)

Double **m** is pronounced as though single and has the effect of stopping nasalisation:

> **femme** (*woman*)
> **pomme** (*apple*)

When **m** is nasalising a vowel, its sound is completely absorbed:

> **chambre** /ʃɑ̃bʀ/ (*room*)
> **faim** /fɛ̃/ (*hunger*)

The phonetic symbols for nasalised vowels are the same whether produced by **m** or **n**. You can tell if a vowel is nasalised by the squiggle (tilde) above it. **M** and **n** both vanish:

> **nom** /nɔ̃/ (*name*)
> **mon** /mɔ̃/ (*my*)

There are three nasalised vowels in French:

> [ɑ̃] **jambe** (*leg*), **temps** (*time*)
> [ɛ̃] **simple** (*plain*), **faim** (*hunger*), **parfum** (*perfume*)
> [ɔ̃] **ombre** (*shade*)

There used to be a fourth one: [œ̃] **parfum** (*perfume*). However, this vowel has been replaced by [ɛ̃] in everyday speech.

There is no nasalisation:

- When **m** is followed by a mute **e**: **rhume** (*cold*), **dame** (*lady*), **Rome**
- When **m** is doubled: **femme** (*woman*), **homme** (*man*)
- When **m** is followed by another vowel and belongs to the next syllable: **a-mi** (*friend*), **a-mour** (*love*), **nu-mé-ro** (*number*)

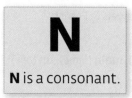

N is a consonant.

 To make the sound: Using the vocal cords to make the sound, press the tip of your tongue against the back of your top teeth (with the sides of your tongue resting against the molars) and let the air out through the nose.

A French **n** is pronounced with the tongue tip against the teeth, whereas an English *n* tends to have the tongue further back against the hard ridge:

> **nuit** (*night*)
> **Nice**
> **nager** (*to swim*)

Double **n** is pronounced without nasalisation. So **bonjour** is nasalised, whilst **bonne nuit** is not:

> **bonne** (*good*)
> **personne** (*person*)
> **anniversaire** (*birthday*)

When **n** is nasalising a vowel, its sound is completely absorbed:

> **centre** /sãtʀ/ (*centre*)
> **volcan** /vɔlkã/ (*volcano*)

The phonetic symbols for nasalised vowels are the same whether produced by **m** or **n**. You can tell if a vowel is nasalised by the squiggle (tilde) above it. **M** and **n** both vanish:

> **mon** /mɔ̃/ (*my*)
> **nom** /nɔ̃/ (*name*)

There are three nasalised vowels in French:

[ɑ̃] **sans** (*without*), **en** (*in*)
[ɛ̃] **vin** (*wine*), **plein** (*full*), **main** (*hand*), **un** (*one*)
[ɔ̃] **onde** (*wave*)

There used to be a fourth one: [œ̃] **parfum** (*perfume*). However, this vowel has been replaced by [ɛ̃] in everyday speech.

There is no nasalisation:

- When **n** is followed by a mute **e** (compare **un** and **une**): **jeune** (*young*), **lune** (*moon*)
- When **n** is doubled: **bonne** (*good*), **panne** (*breakdown*)
- When **n** is followed by another vowel and belongs to the next syllable: **a-ni-mal** (*animal*), **fe-nêtre** (*window*)

O is a vowel.

It has two pronunciations in French.

 To make the sound: The lips fully rounded. The back of the tongue is midway up in the mouth. It is a back vowel.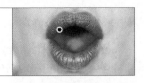

The first is similar to *o* in English *note* as pronounced in a Scottish accent. It is also similar to the *our* in English *four*. It occurs in the following cases:

- When **o** has a circumflex (**ô**): **hôtel** (*hotel*), **côte** (*coast*), **hôpital** (*hospital*)
- When **o** is the final sound of a word (even though it might end with a silent consonant): **numéro** (*number*), **stylo** (*biro*), **nos** (*our*), **mot** (*word*), **trop** (*too much*)

- When **o** is followed by a [z] sound. This is made by **s** sandwiched between two vowels: **rose** (*rose*), **reposer** (*to rest*), **chose** (*thing*)

 A circumflex over the letter **ô** generally indicates that a letter (usually **s**) has been lost over time.

> The letter combination **au** has the same sound [o] as in **beaux** (*beautiful*), **au** (*to*), **eau** (*water*).

 To make the sound: Lips are rounded. The back of the tongue is just below midway in the mouth (lower down than for [o]). It is a back vowel.

It has a shorter sound than [o], as in English *pot*, and tends to occur in closed syllables that end in the sounds [l], [t] and [ʀ].

bol (*bowl*)
votre (*your*)
orange (*orange*)

Nasalised o

 The letter **o** followed by **m** or **n** (in the same syllable) is nasalised. The tongue and mouth position are the same as for [ɔ] but the soft palate is relaxed and lowered to let air out of the nose as well as the mouth:

om: **nom** (*name*), **ombre** (*shade*)
on: **bon** (*good*), **pardon** (*sorry*)

> Doubling **m** or **n** stops nasalisation: **bon** and **nom** (nasalised) but **bonne** and **homme** (not nasalised).

 The [w] sound (similar to the first sound in English *wing*) is produced by **o** in the following combinations:

ou = [u]: **nous** (*we*), **cours** (*lesson*)
oi = [wa]: **roi** (*king*), **soir** (*evening*)

oy + another vowel = [wa]: **voyage** (*trip*), **envoyer** (*to send*)
ou + another vowel = [w]: **oui** (*yes*), **ouest** (*west*)

A 'hardening' vowel

When **o** comes after **c** and **g**, these have [k] and [g] sounds as in **colline** (*hill*) and **gorge** (*throat*). The letter **o** in French (like **a** and **u**) acts as a 'hardening' agent whereas **i**, **e** and **y** are the opposite ('softening' agents).

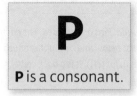

P is a consonant.

[p]   *To make the sound: Press the top lip firmly against the outside edge of the bottom lip and release. The sound* [p] *is made with the breath whereas its voiced twin* [b] *uses vocal cords.*

French **p** is similar to English *p*:

père (*father*)
pour (*for*)
poisson (*fish*)

> The sound [p] is not aspirated in French so try not to let a puff of air escape from your lips when you say it.

In the middle of a word **p** can be silent:

- With **mp** in the same syllable: **temps** (*time*), **champs** (*field*), **compte** (*account*)
- In the words **sept** (*seven*) and **corps** (*body*)

A final **p** is generally silent:

trop (*too much*)

coup (*knock*)
sirop (*syrup*)

Double **p** is pronounced as though single: **frapper** (*to knock*), **appeler** (*to call*), **apporter** (*to bring*)

Ph has the same sound as **f** and both have the same phonetic symbol [f]: **photo** (*photo*), **pharmacie** (*pharmacy*).

In French words beginning **ps**, the **p** is sounded (unlike English): **psychiatrie** (*psychiatry*), **psaume** (*psalm*)

Q is a consonant.

To make the sound: Raise the back of your tongue to touch the roof of your mouth and then release. The sound [k] is made with the breath whereas its voiced twin [g] uses vocal cords.

Q is always found in the combination **qu** which has a [k] sound.

> The sound [k] is not aspirated in French so try not to let out a puff of air when you say it.

Many French question words begin **qu**:

que? (*what?*)
qui? (*who?*)
quel(le)? (*which?*)
quoi? (*what?*)

Qu generally retains this [k] sound wherever it falls in a word:

> **quatre** (*four*)
> **cirque** (*circus*)
> **briquet** (*lighter*)

The **-que** word ending is equivalent to English *-ic* ending:

> **électronique** (*electric*)
> **diabétique** (*diabetic*)

In a few cases **équa-** or **aqua-** have the same [kw] sound as the English equivalents: **équateur** (*equator*), **équation** (*equation*), **aquatique** (*aquatic*)

However, many words containing **qu** which have English equivalents do not have [kw] in French. Examples include **quantité** (*quantity*) and **qualité** (*quality*): both words begin [k].

....

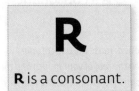

R

R is a consonant.

To make the sound: Raise the back of your tongue close to the back of the throat and make a gargling sound. The sound is made with the vocal cords.

Although some people refer to French **r** as rolled, it is in fact more of a gargled sound like the *ch* in Scottish *loch*. However, the Scottish *ch* sound is not voiced like the French **r**.

> **radio** (*radio*)
> **réserver** (*to book*)
> **riche** (*rich*)

It keeps the same quality in the middle of words:

> **restaurant** (*restaurant*)
> **sourire** (*to smile*)
> **vendre** (*to sell*)

A final **r** is normally pronounced:

> **car** (*because*)
> **sur** (*on*)
> **hiver** (*winter*)
> **sortir** (*to go out*)

However, there are a few cases where a final **r** is not sounded:

- At the end of **-er** verbs: **parler** (*to speak*), **manger** (*to eat*)
- In **-ier** endings: **premier** (*first*), **janvier** (*January*), **papier** (*paper*)

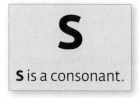

S is a consonant.

French **s** has two pronunciations:

 To make the sound: The end of the tongue is very close to the hard ridge just behind the front teeth forming a narrow airway to force the breath through. The sound [s] is made with the breath whereas its voiced twin [z] uses vocal cords.

The first pronunciation is like the s in English *sun*:

> **salut** (*hi!*)
> **six** (*six*)
> **salade** (*salad*)

The phonetic symbol [s] is the same as for a 'soft' **c** as in **centre** (*centre*) which has the same sound.

Double **s** is sounded as though single:

> **classe** (*class*)
> **aussi** (*also*)

 The second pronunciation is [z] as in English *nose*. This happens when **s** is sandwiched between two vowels:

> **visage** (*face*)
> **rose** (*rose*)
> **maison** (*house*)

A final **s** is normally silent. Therefore adding an **s** to make a word plural doesn't change how it is pronounced:

> **Paris** (*Paris*)
> **jus** (*juice*)
> **la voiture** (*car*)
> **les voitures** (*cars*)

Two common exceptions where the final **s** is pronounced are: **fils** (*son*) and **mars** (*March*).

Note that loan words (words that have been borrowed from another language) are pronounced as they would be in their original language: **bus**, **virus**

 With liaison, a final **s** is pronounced [z]: **le**[z] **enfants** (*children*), **il**[z] **ont** (*they have*)

T is a consonant.

French **t** has two pronunciations:

 To make the sound: Press the point of the tongue firmly against the back of the top teeth and release. The sound [t] uses the breath whereas its voiced twin [d] uses vocal cords.

The first is like English *t* but with the tip of the tongue touching the top teeth, rather than back against the hard ridge, which gives a softer Mediterranean sound:

> **ton** (*your*)
> **trois** (*three*)
> **totalement** (*totally*)

> [t] is not aspirated in French so avoid letting a puff of air escape from your lips when you say it.

It keeps the same quality in the middle of a word:

> **acheter** (*to buy*)
> **montre** (*watch*)

A final **t** is normally silent:

> **mot** (*word*)
> **lait** (*milk*)
> **billet** (*ticket*)

A few exceptions where a final **t** is sounded include: **est** (*east*), **ouest** (*west*), **brut** (*dry*), **net** (*clean*).

Remember that adding **e** will cause a final silent **t** to be sounded. An ending which is silent in the masculine is pronounced when **e** is added to make it feminine:

petit *(m)*→**petite** *(f)* *(small)*
haut *(m)*→**haute** *(f)* *(tall)*

Double **t** is pronounced as though single: **quitter** *(to leave)*, **carotte** *(carrot)*

 The second pronunciation is [s] in the endings **-tion**, **-tiel/-tial** and **-tieux**. The vowel combinations add a 'y' [j] sound:

information *(information)*, **infection** *(infection)*
confidentiel *(confidential)*, **substantiel** *(substantial)*
infectieux *(infectious)*

U is a vowel.

French has two equivalent **u** sounds. On its own it is pronounced [y] as in French **tu**. It also combines with **o** to form **ou** [u] as in French **vous**. The difference between the two sounds is that one is produced at the front of the mouth and the other at the back.

 To make the sound: Round your lips as tightly as possible with the front of the tongue very close to the front of the roof of the mouth. Then say 'ee' [i]. The muscles around the mouth are tense.

Another way to get this sound is by saying *cheese* with the lips spread and gradually bring the side of the lips together to form a tight circle until the sound turns into *choose*. Keep this position of mouth and tongue and practise the following:

une *(one)*
lune *(moon)*
sur *(on top of)*

The phonetic symbol for this sound is [y] which can be confusing.

$[u]$ *To make the sound: Round your lips as tightly as possible with the back of the tongue pulled back toward the back of the mouth.*

The sound [u] is similar to English *oo* as in *pool*, only with rounder lips. The only difference between [y] and [u] is that the tongue is high and forward for [y] and pulled high and back for [u].

Practise moving your tongue backward and forward between the [y] and [u] sounds in **tu** and **vous**.

Other examples of the [u] sound include:

rouge (*red*)
nous (*we*)
cours (*lesson*)

 U [y] followed by another vowel in the same syllable produces a brief sound [ɥ]. Note that this [ɥ] sound is made at the front of the mouth with lips tightly rounded. In the following examples, the English translation often includes a *w*:

ui – **Suisse** (*Swiss*), **suis** (*am*)
ue – **sueur** (*sweat*), **Suède** (*Swede*)

The letter **u** is silent after **q**: **quand** (*when*), **quel** (*which*), **qui** (*who*).

A 'hardening' vowel
When **u** is followed by **c** or **g**, these have a [k] or [g] sound, as in **sécurité** (*security*) and **légume** (*vegetable*). The letter **u** acts as a 'hardening' agent when **g** is followed by **e** or **i** but needs to keep a [g] sound:

long (*m*) → **longue** (*f*) (*long*)

Nasalised u

The letter **u** followed by **m** or **n** (in the same syllable) is nasalised. Previously the vowel sound was [œ̃] but this has been replaced by [ɛ̃]. The tongue and mouth position are the same as for [ɛ] but the soft palate is relaxed and lowered to let air out of the nose as well as the mouth:

un: **un** (*one*)
um: **parfum** (*perfume*)

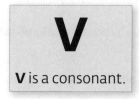

V is a consonant.

To make the sound: Rest your top teeth lightly on your bottom lip and feel them tickling slightly as you make the sound. The sound [v] *uses the vocal cords whereas its voiceless twin* [f] *uses the breath.*

It is similar to English *v*:

voilà! (*there you are!*)
vous (*you*)
vrai (*true*)

It has the same quality in the middle of a word:

travail (*work*)
ouvert (*open*)
Louvre

V is hardly ever a final letter. There is usually an **e** after it. Feminine words ending **-ve** change to **-f** in the masculine:

active (*f*) → **actif** (*m*) (*active*)
sportive (*f*) → **sportif** (*m*) (*sportive*)

The letter **w** is not native to French and is only found in loan words (words borrowed from other languages) such as **Waterloo**, **wagon**, **web**.

As a **w** in a loan word, it retains the sound of the original language:

[v] **wagon**
[w] **web**, **tramway**

The [w] sound is a semivowel. A [w] sound in French is made from the following letter combinations. You may have already come across it in *soiree* (a loan word from French!):

ou – **ouest** (*west*)
oi – **soir** (*evening*), **voiture** (*car*)
oy – **royal** (*royal*), **loyer** (*to rent*)

A similar sound to [w] is [ɥ] which is produced by **u** [y] plus another vowel. Note that this [ɥ] sound is made at the front of the mouth with lips tightly rounded. In the following examples, the English translation often includes a *w*:

ui – **Suisse** (*Swiss*), **suis** (*am*)
ue – **sueur** (*sweat*), **Suède** (*Swede*)

X is a consonant and can be pronounced in four different ways using a combination of sounds:

[ks]

The first pronunciation is as in English *taxi* where **x** is pronounced [ks]:

fixer (*to fix*)
expérience (*experience*)

[gz]

The second pronunciation is as in English *example* where **x** is pronounced [gz]:

exiger (*to demand*)
exhibition (*exhibition*)

[s]

It has an [s] sound in numbers **six** (*six*), **dix** (*ten*) and **soixante** (*sixty*). Be careful with **six** and **dix**. The ending is only sounded when they are on their own. As soon as they are used with a noun, then the final **x** becomes silent (unless there is liaison):

six chambres (*six rooms*)
dix voitures (*ten cars*)

[z]

In the words **deuxième** (*second*), **sixième** (*sixth*) and **dixième** (*tenth*), **x** has a [z] sound.

A final **x** is silent as in English *grand prix* (another French loan word!):

doux (*soft*)
prix (prize)
toux (*cough*)

With liaison, a final **x** is pronounced [z]: **au**[z] **États-Unis** (*to the US*), **deu**[z] **élèves** (*two pupils*)

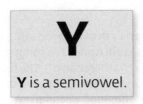

Y is a semivowel.

It has two pronunciations:

 To make the sound: Lips are fully spread and the front of the tongue is raised very close to the front of the roof of the mouth. The muscles around the mouth are tense.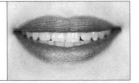

The first sound is as in English *syrup*, where y is a vowel with the same sound as [i]:

y (*there*)   **stylo** (*biro*)   **type** (*type*)

 To make the sound: Raise the middle of your tongue as close to the roof of your mouth as possible without touching it, with the sides of your tongue resting against the sides of your top teeth. The sound is made with the vocal cords.

The second pronunciation is as in English *yellow*. The phonetic symbol for this is [j] which can be confusing. Very few French words begin with **y**. The most common one is **yeux** (*eyes*).

In the middle of a word **y** has two functions. First it modifies the vowel of the first syllable and it is then pronounced [j] at the beginning of the second one:

essayer (*to try*)   **joyeux** (*joyful*)   **payer** (*to pay*)

A [j] sound in French is usually made by the following letter combinations:

- **io**, **ie**, **ia**, **iu**: **radio** (*radio*), **papier** (*paper*), **spécial** (*special*), **aluminium** (*aluminium*)
- **il(l)**: **soleil** (*sun*), **fille** (*daughter*), **travail** (*work*)

Nasalised y

When **y** is followed by **m** or **n** (in the same syllable), it is nasalised and is pronounced as in **vin** (*wine*). The tongue and mouth position are the same as for [ɛ] (rather than [i]). The tongue is forward and slightly lower than halfway up. Lips are slightly spread with the soft palate relaxed and dropped, opening up the nasal cavity to let air out of nose:

sympathique (*likeable*)   **syndicat** (*trade union*)

Z is a consonant.

To make the sound: The end of the tongue is very close to the hard ridge just behind the front teeth forming a narrow airway to force the breath through. The sound [z] uses vocal cords whereas its voiceless twin [s] just uses the breath.

It is pronounced as in English *zoo*:

zéro (*zero*)   **zone** (*zone*)   **gazeux** (*sparkling*)

It keeps the same quality in the middle of a word:

bizarre (*strange*)   **bronzage** (*suntan*)

At the end of the word **z** is silent:

chez (*at home*)   **riz** (*rice*)   **nez** (*nose*)